I TOLD YOU NOT TO GO THERE!

Written by JT Holton

Illustrations by Jason G Corre

Edited by Laura J Holton

Copyright 2019
All rights reserved
ISBN: 978-1-78972-299-4
Printed in the UK

Bizarre, outrageous, and often unbelievable — an exploration of the world of online travel reviews.

Featuring illustrations to bring these stories to life, with only the slightest bit of exaggeration!

Introduction

Travelling the world can be immensely rewarding: expanding one's horizons and opening the mind to acquire a deeper understanding of our beautiful planet and all the amazing creatures who inhabit it.

On the other hand, if you make all the wrong planning decisions, travel can be the source of enormous frustration, disgusting experiences, and even physical or mental distress.

But, as with most things in the modern age, the internet has come to the rescue. With literally millions of online reviews, for virtually every hotel, restaurant, and tourist attraction in the world, available at the click of a button, travellers now have instant access to all the information they could possibly need to plan their trip of a lifetime.

In the olden days, people looking for a bit of adventure or just a relaxing break would visit one of their many local travel agents. You would gather up a big stack of travel brochures (who needs trees?) and read the glowing descriptions of the fabulous places you could visit. After browsing through all the lovely-sounding holiday destinations, you would wander back down to the travel agent and pay the deposit for your dream trip.

That was it — everything was settled and all that was left was to wait, with great anticipation, for the date of your vacation to finally arrive.

Of course, it didn't always work out perfectly, as the only information you had about your fantastic holiday was derived from the sales pitch in the travel brochure. Could you trust it to be 100% honest and accurate?

I remember a winter skiing holiday my partner and I took to a beautiful-looking hotel in a small Austrian town. We were rather poor and needed to get the maximum value from our limited funds. We found a surprisingly good price at a hotel that was described as being "five minutes from the town" — it sounded perfect.

Naively, we made the huge mistake of assuming this meant a five-minute walk. But no... it was five minutes in an off-road 4x4 driven at breakneck speed from the pickup point in the town. Obviously management had clearly been through this experience before and needed to prove that the hotel was, in fact, only five minutes from town.

However, if we needed to walk into town for a meal or some evening entertainment, it was more like an hour's trudge through the snow in the freezing cold.

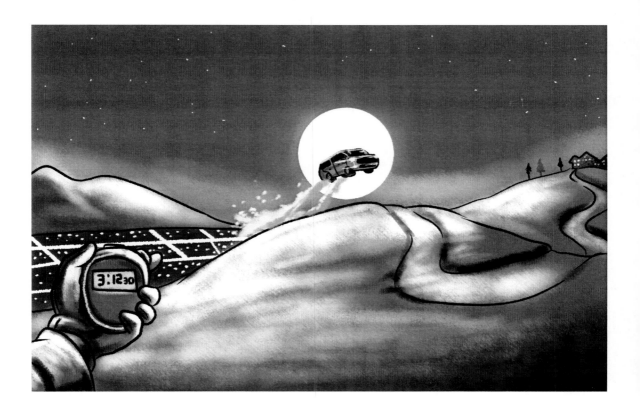

But that wasn't the worst of it. The really big surprise was regarding the bathroom facilities at the hotel. We had booked a cheaper room, clearly described as not having an en suite bathroom. No problem — I didn't mind walking down the hall to use a shared bathroom. But no... the brochure didn't say anything about shared bathrooms — and in fact, there weren't any in the hotel. We soon learned how sweaty and smelly two human beings can become after a week of skiing with no bath or shower facilities.

The essential point here is that the brochure did not lie. The hotel was five minutes from the town (when driven by a madman in Land Rover) and the room did not provide en suite bathing facilities (or, for that matter, any bathing facilities!).

But wouldn't it have been extremely useful if we could have received some frank and, if appropriate, critical information from people who had actually stayed in this hotel? Then we could have been pre-warned about these very unpleasant shortcomings.

Of course, not everyone was happy to book their holiday trips through travel agents in those days. The more independent-minded travellers would make their own arrangements after pouring through recommendations in travel guidebooks.

Generally, this was my preferred way to travel and I would deeply study multiple guidebooks to get the best possible advice about where to go, where to stay, and where to eat. Each guidebook would contain a vast array of recommendations for every place I was planning to visit, so I could easily make the ideal choices for hotels, restaurants, tourist attractions, etc.

However, could the writers of the guidebook honestly have had time to stay in each of the hotels they recommended and eat in every restaurant they raved about?

I don't think so — at least not every year. This meant that recommendations were often derived from second-hand reports, and much of the information was in danger of being uselessly out of date.

Then along came the internet and all our travel problems were solved. Now, we can get first-hand reports and recommendations about every hotel, restaurant, tourist attraction, and guided tour in every part of the world.

Perfect! What could possibly go wrong?

Logically, we recognize that average people contributing their insights and observations to websites like TripAdvisor, Hotels.com, Google, Facebook, etc. are not professional travel writers. That's understandable, and it should be acceptable. We can live with their limited literary skills and numerous spelling mistakes. We just want their honest opinions about places they have personally visited. Then, we can make informed judgments to create our own perfect travel plans.

We also recognize that everyone has different standards and expectations that are bound to affect the ratings in their reviews. That's all right — we can deal with that. Just give us your frank opinions and let us know whether this is one of the most wonderful hotels in the world or a Fawlty Towers tribute act.

Of course, there is also the risk that a hotel or restaurant review might be a complete phony — possibly written by the friends of the proprietor in the hopes of boosting his business's position in the online rankings. Or, from a more sinister perspective, a review could be written by a nasty competitor who hopes his business will benefit if his competitor appears to offer a shoddy service and a rude attitude. These bogus reviews can definitely be problematic — at least in theory.

But most of us convince ourselves that we can easily see through these sham reviews written by imposters. We're clever enough to wade through all the available information and make wise decisions that will ensure a perfect trip.

Having used online review sites extensively in recent years to plan my own travel adventures, I have come across a number of bizarre, and sometimes shocking, reports about hotels, restaurants, and other tourist destinations. These valuable contributions from fellow travellers have certainly helped me to avoid many potentially disastrous mistakes.

Now, I could lie and say that my motivation for writing this book is to perform some sort of public service to warn other people about horrible places they should avoid. But, to be honest, perhaps the real purpose of this book is just to make you feel that your latest disappointing trip wasn't actually so bad after all — it could have been a real nightmare!

Some of the Worst Places in the World

Of course, there are some truly disgusting places in the world. Online reviews provide a great way for travellers to warn others about the really appalling hotels and restaurants they have stumbled across in their adventures. When it comes to hotels, the usual array of nasty features frequently come up: filthy carpets, smelly bathrooms, cigarette burns in bedspreads, blood stains and other suspicious fluids on sheets, as well as the sound of other guests shouting, crying, chanting, or even just breathing through paper-thin walls.

But, by wading through reviews of the world's worst hotels and restaurants, it is always impressive to see that some establishments go above and beyond the standards required to achieve a one-star review and provide some unique assets to ensure they stand out at the bottom of any list of miserable experiences.

The following quotes from online reviews certainly don't encourage me to visit any of these places:

"When I got off the train and told the cab driver where I'm going he looked at me as if I was crazy... The 'receptionist' sits behind bullet proof glass.... Need I say more?"

"Room description said it had a bathtub - but all it had was a bucket to pour over my head for a shower. They should have simply said it had a shower!"

"The mini-bar in our room only contained two dirty glasses and a coating of grime."

"The restaurant's "free breakfast" consisted of last night's cold pizza and beans."

"The cockroach (dead!) in our corridor was there on arrival and still in residence on departure."

"If you go to Detroit, get arrested and spend the night in jail, it will be better than this place."

"I called the desk to ask what's the problem, he told me "You have to open the door, because the previous guest smoked in the room and the smoke is affecting the wifi"

"The area wasn't very nice and seems to suffer from a lot of crime. We came back one evening to find our car had been broken into and the steering wheel had been ripped right out of the car! That was obviously disappointing."

"There was a pornographic DVD in the player in our room which at one point staff burst into the room to retrieve."

"At night all we could hear was people yelling downstairs, the street that this hotel is located on is extremely busy and you will hear people outside your window most of the night. Even though the people outside were annoying, the hotel staff was even worse, we had to listen to the staff yelling at each other at 3 in the morning."

Although the reviewer above is extremely negative and gives an overall rating of one star, it's great that he recognizes this is a very cheap hotel and gives it three stars for value!

"When I got there this guy was having a gun brawl outside. I tried to quickly leave but the waiter grabbed my collar and forced me to eat here. The food was terrible and overpriced.

The next day I filed a police report. I will never go back here again."

"The room was ridiculously small, the lighting made a cave seem bright, the water was brown (I'm not kidding!) and foul-smelling, the mattress must have been scavenged from a city dump, and the carpet so dirty I wouldn't walk on it without wearing somebody else's shoes."

"...we found a cigarette butt under our bed, but unfortunately we do not smoke"

"When we were shown to our room I was surprised to see that it was located by the kitchen and restaurant separated only by a glass sliding door and curtain. I was advised by the staff not to worry because we would only be woken at 6:00am when the kitchen started preparing!

Great way to enjoy a relaxing holiday, being woken at 6:00am every day. But I suppose I do feel sorry for the people trying to enjoy a meal and getting a glimpse of my naked butt through the gap in the curtain"

Sometimes a terrible hotel receives the occasional 5-star review. Very often, these are just fake reviews posted by the manager or his friends.

Nonetheless, some people really seem to enjoy the excitement of staying in a dodgy and dangerous hotel.

How about this 5-star review, titled: *"Adventure in Detroit!"*

"This place is not for the weak or easily frightened, but we had no problems there..."

But sometimes a hotel is so bad you just want to somehow survive through the night and get out of there:

"The sheets were dirty, to be on the safe side I slept on top of them with my clothes on. I can't even describe the carpet, seems like a murder took place here."

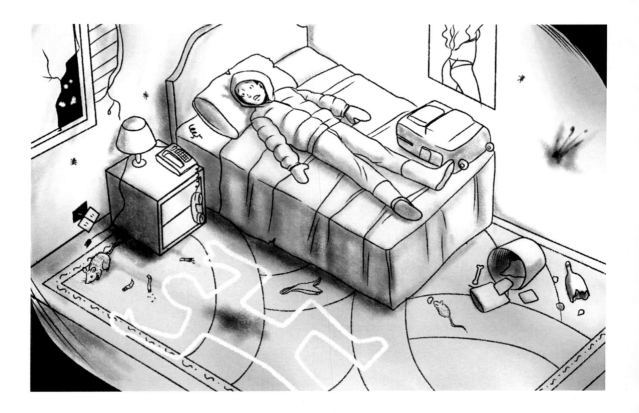

Challenging Places to Visit

There are some interesting but troubled locations around the world where you can't necessarily expect all the facilities to be top notch.

<u>Chernobyl</u>
Who would expect to find a restaurant inside the exclusion zone around the site of the world's biggest nuclear accident? At least this reviewer provides readers with some assurances that the food should be safe to eat:

"All food is scorched from outside the exclusion zone"

<u>North Korea</u>
You might expect more from a so-called '6-star' hotel — but this is Pyongyang:

"I wouldn't even allow my pets to stay here. I would rather sleep outside (although not in the winter)."

"There is no service, padlocks on the fire escapes, no showers, no water or electricity most days but who cares you'll be out in a week if you behave yourself!"

Of course, not every hotel in Pyongyang is a complete disappointment. The number one rated hotel in the city can certainly provide some excitement:

"When dinner was finished we made our way back to the lifts and waited with a large group to get in the lift. Around 20 people from a Russian group squeezed into the lift, the doors shuddered shut and slowly started rising. When it reached the 5th floor, you heard a whooshing noise and the floor numbers flashing down back to 0, where the door shuddered open and the group inside looked white as a sheet as the lift had just fallen from the 5th floor.

I climbed up 64 flights of stairs that night in the dark (yep, no emergency lighting, but hey, it's North Korea)."

<u>Big Cities in the Developing World</u>
All big cities around the world are bound to have some terrible hotels. Checking the reviews for some of the lowest-rated hotels in these cities can reveal some shocking deficiencies.

All the same, the criticisms can sometimes seem a bit trivial.

For a low-budget hotel in Mumbai, you might expect worse comments than this in a one-star review:

"The TV wasn't working, but they didn't give a damn."

But this shortcoming obviously bothered the reviewer immensely, leading to a rather over-the-top conclusion:

"the guy at reception is arrogant and probably the worst person living on the planet."

Of course, the great value of online review sites is that unfortunate customers can warn others to avoid their horrible experiences. I think this is summed up well at the end of a long, very negative review of an awful hotel somewhere in Central Africa:

"Overall it was a terrible experience. I can only hope to someday erase it from my memory, but you can avoid it completely if you please listen to my warnings."

How to Achieve Nearly Unanimous One-Star Reviews

Let's face it, most people still don't read reviews before they book a hotel. So who cares if your hotel gets one star in the vast majority of its reviews? This is at least amusing for diligent travellers who do read the reviews and it makes them feel very superior for not being stupid enough to stay at your hotel.

One hotel in London has managed to receive a one-star rating in more than 70% of its reviews.

Perhaps they should provide a checklist to help other hotel managers achieve a similar level of distinction:

- ✓ Install a noisy refrigerator in the room and make sure it is pre-loaded with a moldy, half-eaten sandwich.
- ✓ Make sure the duvet cover has sufficient cigarette burn holes and suspicious-looking yellow stains.
- ✓ Provide pillows that reviewers will describe as "paper thin – like a sheet of A4".
- ✓ Charge an extortionate rate to convince customers that your hotel must be good.
- ✓ Install mousetraps under the beds — it's a wonderful treat for guests when the traps go off in the middle of the night.
- ✓ Leave a cigarette butt floating in the toilet to greet new arrivals.
- ✓ And please ensure there are adequate dusty surfaces to allow patrons to leave messages for the next unfortunate guests.

Can You Believe It?

Sometimes, it's a bit hard to believe the claims people make in their reviews:

"Don't book your car with them. The car they rented us didn't shift out of first, no seat belts and the windows didn't close so the seats were soaked from the pouring rain."

"While away from our room people came in to the bungalows to take chairs and furniture without telling us for a party they were having and broke the railing in our bungalow."

"I found a cat's paw in my pillowcase"

But at least this reviewer gave the place five stars for "Location". And he didn't seem too concerned about possibly finding the rest of the cat somewhere else in the room.

"My boyfriend took me here for a celebration - after an average meal (not at an average price) we returned home to a voicemail asking us to return the salt and pepper pots."

That seems like a rather outrageous accusation for a restaurant to make. Nonetheless, the reviewer doesn't actually claim that they didn't take the salt and pepper pots!

"Enthusiastically I bit into my baked potato - CRUNCH! - I was horrified to find a rusty screw inside the potato!"

"My girlfriend and I were having a romantic meal but suddenly the mood was ruined when one of the staff spit into my hair."

Some People Just Can't Be Helped

The shocking thing about the reviews of obviously terrible hotels and restaurants is that some people are willing to ignore an uninterrupted string of one-star reviews and take a chance despite the horrors reported by previous guests.

"I read the reviews about the bad service & food, still insisting to try it!"

Unfortunately, the restaurant lived up to the previous reviews so this customer added another one-star review.

"we weren't sure about booking after seeing the previous reviews" — (10 out of 12 one-star reviews)

Unsurprisingly, they hated it!

And from a review titled *"Undoubtedly the worst hotel in the world"*:

"Stayed out of curiousity as I've heard the really horrible reputation of it. The rooms are small dirty and stinky. It's beyond just dirty. I rather live on the streets than stay in this piece of doodoo of a hotel again."

Interesting — this customer was "curious" to find out if this genuinely was the worst hotel in the world. Good to hear that he was able to confirm it for himself.

While it's understandable that some people might ignore the bad experiences other people describe in their reviews, you would hope that people could at least learn from their own bad experiences. This is from a one-star review for a budget motel:

"Rooms are small, loud, and very basic. WiFi will not connect, don't even try..

This hotel is basically a dump!"

So this is obviously a place to avoid. But then the reviewer reveals that he seems to be one of their most loyal customers:

"We've stayed here 4 times in 10 years, and there's never any improvement!" — Some people can't even help themselves!

Cafés and restaurants in Venice are renowned for being ridiculously expensive. They mainly deal with tourists who they will never see again, so why not overcharge for drinks, using menus without prices? Sites like TripAdvisor are great for identifying such rip-off joints, but who has time to consult online reviews when looking for a café for a quick drink when you're busy sightseeing around Venice?

All the same, some people use rather questionable logic when choosing a restaurant without the benefit of online reviews:

"It looked a little run down so we thought we might get away with good local food at reasonable prices."

This particular restaurant has managed to receive 88% one-star reviews, so no, they didn't get 'good local food at reasonable prices' — and the restaurant received another one-star review.

Why Do People Visit Places They Really Should Avoid?

It is always rather puzzling to me as to why some people visit an attraction even though they have absolutely no interest in the potential appeal of the place. And then they proceed to post a terrible online review.

A classic example of this is a negative review about a fabulous beach:

"It's a great beach, just too sandy"

And it's not just the sand on beaches that some people hate:

"No one told us there would be fish in the sea. The children were startled!"

Some people seem to be surprised when they arrive at their overseas holiday destination only to discover that they have actually gone to another country:

"We went on holiday to Spain and had a problem with the taxi drivers as they were all Spanish."

Even worse:

"There are too many Spanish people. The receptionist speaks Spanish. The food is Spanish. Too many foreigners now live abroad!" — I'm not making this up!

<u>National Gallery - London</u>
"Went on a guided tour and all they did was talk about paintings - boring!"

<u>Review of a Chinese Restaurant:</u>
"Disappointed by this place. the food was too 'chinese'."

Three-Hour Botanical Garden Walking Tour
"It was VERY unsuitable for people who had difficulty walking"

Kalalau Trail in Hawaii

One of my favorite hikes in the world. A bit challenging, but hikers are rewarded with spectacular views throughout the trail.

A total of 83% of reviewers give this trail five stars — but this hike is obviously not for everyone:

"Overall I wouldn't recommend it for kids or people who don't enjoy hiking."

"Now mind if you like to hike and like waterfalls you will probably like it. We hated it."

Grand Canyon

Although it is clearly one of the most popular and spectacular tourist destinations in the world, the Grand Canyon certainly doesn't satisfy everyone:

"Very disappointing 5 hour drive for a hole in the ground."

"Not recommended for anyone who wants to go because the trip is very tiring. And there is not enough to do for those who have no aptitude for walking."

"Very dull and boring. Not a lot to see and loads of selfie sticks ready to take your eye out! Don't waste your time or money on this its just not worth it."

"A bit of a waste of a day I'm afraid. If you've seen pictures you've seen it. Definitely a case of the emperor's new clothes. If enough people say it's good then others follow the lead and ignore the reality. Don't waste your time."

"Couldn't see what all the fuss is about. Dragged here by the missus when I should have been playing golf. It's just a hole in the ground. A big hole, mind."

The review above received 14 helpful votes!

Review Title: *"Nature is Crap"*

"I've been to a number of so called landmarks in my time - but what the hell was this? Just an overblown sandy ditch. Really don't get the fascination! Took two hours to get there – should've stayed in my hotel and watched a DVD instead..."

Another 14 helpful votes for this review!

Stonehenge

How about these comments from a bored visitor to the ancient and world-famous stone circle:

"I personally have no interest in any stones in the ground. Just wanted to get back to the hotel so I could have a few beers while watching the darts on TV."

Angkor Wat, Cambodia

"Boring...It's just a bunch of fancy rocks on top of other fancy rocks, inside a hot jungle. I mean if you're into that kind of thing, sure. I prefer American rocks"

Hot Air Balloon Ride

There aren't many things more exhilarating than a ride in a hot air balloon: silently floating above the earth to marvel at the beautiful scenery below you. For many people, this is a magical, once-in-a-lifetime experience. But the activity isn't necessarily for everyone:

"There was no sign telling you that you shouldn't get on the hot air balloon ride if you're afraid of heights."

People Are the Real Problem

If researching for this book has taught me anything, it's that many hotels, restaurants, and tourist attractions could operate very happily if they just didn't have to put up with people!

Some People Are Just Too Picky
We would all like our holidays to be great, but can we reasonably expect that everything will be absolutely perfect?

"There was no egg-slicer in the apartment!"

At a charming restaurant, where I personally have enjoyed a delicious meal, one reviewer was a bit too obsessed about the colour of the beer.

"We asked for a blonde beer and the bartender assured us he had a good one. But as he starting poring the beer, he admitted it was more amber than blonde!"

Outrageous! Of course this earned a one-star review.

"Our party was large so we needed to have two tables pushed together. But there was at least 3cm difference between the height of the two tables!"

"We had booked and paid in advance for a queen size bed but what we got was two single beds of differing heights pushed together."

Accessibility Issues

Sometimes, reviewers raise what initially seem to be legitimate concerns about an establishment. In a review titled "Accessibility Issues", you can expect that the reviewer is going to point out important shortcomings of a hotel that may cause problems for some guests; for example, those using a wheelchair.

"There's a flight of stairs to enter the hotel and another to access rooms."

The first sentence clearly warns potential guests that this hotel may not be easy to enter for some people. However, it soon becomes clear that this isn't the "accessibility issue" the reviewer is actually complaining about:

"The room was gorgeous and spacious, with a comfortable four poster bed and plenty of seating. But the main reason I'm not giving 5 stars is that the entrance to the shower and width of the tub in our room were both extremely narrow-- my hips and shoulders were too wide to step up into the shower, so I had to awkwardly shimmy in sideways."

Is this truly the fault of the hotel, or is it possible that someone needs to show a bit more restraint at the breakfast buffet?

Operator Error: Booking the Wrong Dates
"So we had a booking in this splendid hotel. A place we have been before. Kids are excited to go and we just want 24 hours of fun.

Then we made a mistake and our dates were booked wrong."

Their weekend away was ruined and they needed to blame someone other than themselves. Giving the hotel a one-star review somehow made them feel better.

Operator Error: Visiting on a Bad Day
Is it fair to give a one-star review when you simply visited on the wrong day?

"We drove the hour to the lookout point during a drizzly day--and were disappointed that the sight was completely fogged in."

<u>...Or Not Visiting at All!</u>
"Long story short, my card was not charged, but the (last) room was given to another party that apparently was on the reservation system at the same time as I was."

So he gave them a one-star review — of course!

"We saw this on the website and decided to make a visit. When we arrived we were told that scheduled trips ran at 8.30 and 1.00pm and that they were fully booked that day" — so they gave it a one-star review.

One of the top restaurants in Paris just received its first one-star review. What was the customer's criticism? Well, actually he freely admitted that he has never been to the restaurant. He was suspicious about so many glowingly positive reviews being written by people who have not submitted many other reviews. So he just thought he would balance things out by giving the restaurant its very first one-star review.

Thanks, that's very helpful!

Operator Error: Lacking Self-Control

This is one of the most extreme examples of "operator error" in a hotel review. I think the unhappy guest may need to take some degree of responsibility for what happened on her holiday:

"My fiancé and I booked a twin-bedded room but we were placed in a double-bedded room.

We now hold you responsible for the fact that I find myself pregnant. This would not have happened if you had put us in the room we booked."

Sometimes, It's Just a Difference of Opinion

A very highly-rated boutique hotel in Cape Town finally received its first one-star review after more than a thousand extremely positive reviews. The guests in this case were traumatized by waking up in the middle of the night to find a big nasty "rat" in their room. They called the front desk and the creature was trapped in the bathroom and quickly removed.

Obviously, encountering a rat in your hotel room can be very disturbing, and it's understandable that you would be upset and might write a negative review. Nevertheless, there was clearly a strong difference of opinion as to whether the offending animal was indeed a rat — or simply a harmless little mouse.

To further complicate matters, the hotel owner claimed that the guests had left their window wide open with a big wedge of cheese sitting on the table.

But, the big question is: was it really a scary "rat" or just a cute little "mouse"?

Perhaps the suspects need to appear in a police lineup.

What Were You Expecting?

Some people end up disappointed due to their own unreasonable expectations. This can sometimes be due to very literal interpretations of other people's descriptions.

This reviewer obviously wasn't moved by the ancient stone circle:

"We heard it was a magical place but there was no evidence of magic on our visit. Also, another review said the stones had energy - but we didn't see them move at all."

Sometimes, visitors just don't understand what they should expect to see at world-famous historical sites.

One reviewer was obviously looking for something quite different from his visit to the ancient Roman Baths:

"Way too expensive for what you see. I was hoping to see some "romans" going about their bathing (might have livened it up a bit) but no luck."

Is this reviewer being sarcastic or just stupid about what he expected to see outside the world's most famous recording studio?

"I was told to check out the zebras crossing Abbey Road whilst in London but I didn't see any. Perhaps you have to come at night to see them. There were lots of people there looking for them but didn't see a single one! I'd recommend London Zoo at Regent's Park over Abbey Road for zebras."

Another visitor to the famous zebra crossing found that it just wasn't tacky enough for him:

"My disappointment in not finding street sellers, either side of the road, selling cheap t-shirts and merchandise was a surprise."

You always want to ensure you are going to be welcome when you go somewhere abroad. But these people may be just a bit paranoid:

"The brochure stated: 'No hairdressers at the accommodation'. We're trainee hairdressers and were concerned about whether we would be OK staying there"

We All Have Different Priorities

For some people, seeing masses of people on a beach is a sign that it must be a fantastic beach — otherwise, there wouldn't be so many people there. Other people are looking for a remote and secluded beach where they can enjoy some peace and solitude.

One of my favorite places in the world is a stunning, isolated beach on the island of Barbados. But this type of seclusion doesn't appeal to everyone:

"Its one of those places that if you were drowning, no one would hear you scream for help."

Most often, people have very legitimate complaints that lead them to write negative reviews. Other times, a traveller may be disappointed by something that most of us would not see as being necessarily bad. Case in point, a one-star review titled:

"I did not see any cockroaches".

When couples travel together, it's not always easy for both of them to enjoy the same experience. One female reviewer complained just that, whereas her husband may have had a very different viewpoint:

"Topless sunbathing on the beach should be banned. The holiday was ruined as my husband spent all day looking at other women."

In many cases, you can't please either the husband or wife. One couple had a particularly upsetting experience in India:

"The elephants we saw on our honeymoon were visibly aroused which made my wife upset and made me feel inadequate."

You Can't Please Everyone

After visiting some amazing places in my travels, I occasionally go back and check the latest reviews just to remind myself how lucky I was to have such great experiences. However, I often find that even the most wonderful places in the world can't please everyone:

Eco Lodge in the Central American Jungle
Although hundreds of reviewers almost unanimously rave about this magical place, some people still find a way to be miserable:

"so we went canoeing up the river to the next jungle lodge hoping to go there for lunch – at the first rapids the canoe capsized, there is no warning as such about the rapids. Capsizing was not too scary – however we did both lose our brand new iPhones due to water damage! So it was an expensive free boat trip!"

Perhaps next time you go canoeing up a jungle river, you might like to leave the brand new iPhones behind?

<u>Lovely Boutique Hotel in New Zealand</u>
Here is a comment taken from one of the (very rare) poor reviews of this beautiful little hotel:

"at one point my mum watched me sleeping in my room, from her balcony"

Is this actually the fault of the hotel or does this reviewer possibly have an issue with his mother that he needs to resolve?

<u>Wildlife Sanctuary</u>
If you visit a wildlife rescue centre, wouldn't you expect the treatment of animals to be a very high priority? Apparently, not everyone shares that opinion:

"Animals are important, however, not as important as humans. I have some minor opinions about things like Sea World and it's treatment of animals, but these guys are extreme on the side of animals."

<u>Beautiful Country Pub in England</u>
One of the very few negative reviews for this pub complains about the unfriendly attitude of management:

"one of the managers came outside into the front garden where we were sitting with a group of kids and adults and were told the children are NOT allowed to run around in the garden!!!!"

The manager quite reasonably replied:

*"**We do not have a front garden** and we feel it is inappropriate for children to be allowed to run around in our car park and front porch".*

New Zealand Jet Boat Ride

With more than 90% five-star reviews, this attraction is clearly very exciting. Still, you can't please everyone. The sole one-star review simply says: *"Not fast enough"*

Some Places May Be Great, But They Admittedly Have Their Flaws

Gourmet Italian Ice Cream Shop in Florida
In my personal opinion, this place has the best ice cream in the world, served in freshly-made waffle cones. However, it's just a very simple shop without any atmosphere and a proprietor who seems to piss a lot of people off. A total of 67% of reviews (including mine) give this place 5 stars. Nonetheless, not everyone is satisfied — 9% of reviewers give a one-star rating. Do they have legitimate complaints?

*"The man behind the counter gives me a death stare, an 'I want to kill you'. We asked for samples and were told **no samples**."*

They never tried the ice cream, but they submitted a one-star review because they didn't get a free sample.

Another reviewer received a much stronger response when he asked for a free sample:

"he said to me in a threatening tone of voice, 'You know I am from Long Island and I have brought tears to the eyes of plenty of tough guys and gangsters in my life'"

Five-Star Boutique Hotel in South Africa
"we weren't very happy that the window in our bathroom connected directly with the dining room of the restaurant"

You might think this item should have been included in the earlier "Can You Believe It?" section. However, I've actually had the pleasure of staying in this hotel and can confirm that the bathroom window in one of the guest rooms honestly does connect directly to the dining room!

Responses from Management

After bad reviews are published, it's important to note whether management cares enough to bother responding. If management never responds to negative reviews, this sends a clear message that they just don't give a damn — and will continue to rely on business from customers who don't take the time to do any research.

But what can a company representative say in response to reviews from obviously disappointed, and sometimes angry, customers? In response to a long and detailed review describing a customer's terrible experience at a hotel on a honeymoon trip, one manager's flippant response was to simply say:

"Congratulations on your honeymoon! Thank you for staying with us at the Paradise Hotel and for your feedback."

It always shows a bit of class when the manager provides a dignified response to a harsh review.

The title of one extremely negative hotel review stated that the place:

"Looks like a building from Chernobyl"

The manager wisely chose to rise above this insult:

"Unfortunately when a review starts by comparing the hotel to one of the greatest man made disasters and loss of innocent life of the twentieth century I am unsure as to how my efforts to find a resolution would have proceeded".

Of course, the most entertaining responses come from frustrated and grumpy proprietors who have had enough and decide to make feeble excuses or even accusations about the customer. These responses certainly don't reflect well on the establishment, but they can give potential customers a useful insight into management's attitude.

For instance, it doesn't make a great impression when a B&B proprietor responds to a critical review using the signature "kickass-manager".

"Out of our window was a collection of old sinks, a toilet and bath tub."

Management's response:

"We believe the hotel is a charming place to stay, it's not modern, chic and surrounded by perfect concrete - we leave that to the inner city hotels which have no character! :)"

Sometimes, the manager has a very different recollection about an incident than the customer:

"'I'm sorry that you didn't receive the service that you expected. When I spoke with you the first time, I was under the impression that you were mad at your husband for dead-bolting you out of the room. I did ask you if there was anything that we could do and you yelled "NO!"

Spelling mistakes and bad grammar don't make for a particularly positive impression in a review. For some proprietors, these shortcomings are an indication that the reviewer does not deserve to be taken seriously:

"We won't take any lessons from such an obvious low life as you until you learn to use proper sentence construction like a normal adult. Meaningless colloquialisms, lack of capital letters and a total absence of full stops indicate someone who is not fit to pass judgement on a goldfish. You will continue to be served drinks in a plastic cup with a 'no spill' top until you stop writing like a five year old."

"The really disappointing thing is your inability to spell the word 'disappointing' in your disappointingly lame headline. Must do better."

"Not sure who was using the family brain cell when this literary masterpiece was penned, but it looks like it was written by a five year old. If there was any hair in your food, then it must have been one of your own and was probably the main reason for any grease on your plate. Maybe the piece of metal was one of your fillings, which could have shot out, when you were talking with your mouth full."

It can be a daunting challenge to respond to critical reviews. Management needs to appear sensitive to the reviewers' complaints but must also defend the establishment and give readers a positive impression about their commitment to customer service.

If they honestly want to take this challenge seriously, they need to engage a professional Public Relations Manager to respond to reviews.

The following responses are all from the Public Relations Manager of one restaurant, which has been prone to receive quite a few critical reviews:

"Just what we don't need - an arrogant, belligerent, loudmouth with undercooked, soggy opinions on just about every topic they know absolutely nothing about. The only thing that has melded together in one great soggy lump is your brain, but after a quick lobotomy with a plastic fork, you should be alright once we have stored your frontal lobes in a styrofoam box. How's that for sustainability people?"

"It doesn't take a genius to order fish and chips, but it would seem in your case even this simple task is beyond your capabilities - "Less than average" should be tattooed on your forehead."

"Try sitting properly without your elbows and knees jutting out and you might have a better dining experience. Giving us a one star rating because you are too big to fit into a standard seat is an absolute disgrace."

"I'm not sure if you were sober when you penned this literary masterpiece, but you have written complete and utter gibberish. If you continue with this course of action, your girlfriend will ditch you, your family will disown you and you'll be sacked from your job. Shape up before it's too late."

With the growing influence of online review sites these days, some managers choose to respond to a potential negative review before the customer has even considered writing it:

"I had a dish of the day posted with accompanying linguini. I was served spaghetti. I point it out to the waitress, very friendly. In compensation, I ask if you can offer me coffee. Faced with the refusal, I declare simply wanting to settle and leave. Everything could have stopped there.

But at the moment of settling, the boss of the establishment approaches me and declares me "if I find the least comment about the linguini on trip advisor, I will find you!" Not wanting to disappoint this lady, so I downloaded the application only to share its sense of hospitality.

It goes without saying that linguini are not a big deal, but that threats are one of them. I thank her very much for blowing me the idea!"

Proprietors Must Get Exasperated
The worst review one B&B has ever received gave it three stars. Still, that was obviously too critical for the owner:

"Sometimes you are wondering what kind of people these modern times and the Internet rear. Perhaps e.g. those, who just like the cheap sensation to complain from a safe, unassailable position, although there is nothing to complain about."

It's always refreshing to see a proprietor who makes a serious effort to defend his establishment's excellent reputation. A very highly-regarded whisky bar in Glasgow received a rare one-star review from an obviously very impatient customer.

The manager of the bar took the time and effort to review the CCTV footage to verify the accuracy of this reviewer's complaints about slow service:

"You put your foot on our front door step at 13:32:03
You finally came to the bar at 13:32:51
You turned away from the bar at 13:33:11
You took your foot off our front door step at 13:33:18

So all told you spent 20 seconds waiting at the bar in a visit that lasted a minute and a quarter.

The youngest Scotch we sell waits three years in cask before its even considered a whisky, let alone ready to be bottled. The oldest whisky we have waited 50 years before being bottled. When it went into cask, no-one knew who Sergeant Pepper was and the UK was trying to get INTO Europe.

If you feel 20 seconds is too long in your life to hang on in that company, then maybe you're not ready for whisky yet. We'll be happy to help you with recommendations when you are."

And then there are times when management just can't take any more abuse and respond in the only reasonable way:

"There are three men over the age of forty working in the hotel. Only one of them was working on the night you stayed, so we didn't know how to deal with the 'grumpy old men' in your review, until my assistant manager came up with the only viable solution. We've decided to execute all three of these men to ensure that no other guests will have to endure the horrific ordeal you went through that evening in the bar.

Paul, Martin and Luis will be blindfolded and shot in the back of the head at Fitz's cross after mass this Sunday. There will be trad music, cocktail sausages and face-painting for the kids and I can organise a pair of complimentary tickets for you if you wish to attend. I know this will not make up for what happened to you but we hope it will go some way towards showing you that we take your feedback seriously."

Honesty Is the Best Policy

To avoid receiving bad reviews, it's always helpful when owners are honest about what they are offering to prevent any unwarranted high expectations: *"Those wishing to stay at the Hans Brinker Budget Hotel, Amsterdam, do so at their own risk and will not hold the hotel liable for food poisoning, mental breakdowns, terminal illness, lost limbs, radiation poisoning, certain diseases associated with the 18th century, plague."*

A Bit of Wit is Always Appreciated

The main purpose of a negative review may be to warn other people, so they can avoid repeating your bad experience. But it's definitely more entertaining when complaining guests show a bit of wit in their reviews:

"The room had an air-conditioner that sounded like a little kid banging on a steel kettle all night. I should have saved my money, slept on the street and paid a tramp to bang a steel kettle all night."

"The location leaves a lot to be desired, unless you happen to be a free-lance exotic dancer. Nestled in a district of sex shops and strip clubs, the area attracts the sort of

people that you would cross the street to avoid. As you enter the hotel, you are greeted by decor that is almost medieval - and a strange old man who is always angry; and ironically smoking a cigar next to the 'no smoking' sign.

Next, you enter the lift - I have seen suicide attempts that adhere to more health and safety measures. Seriously - take the stairs. It rather optimistically has a four person maximum capacity - God help you if one of your companions happens to be fat..."

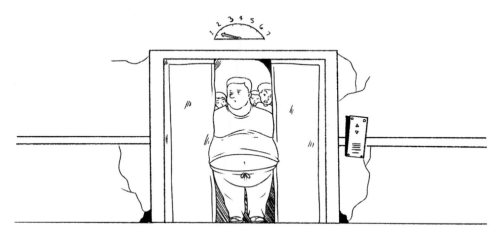

There's Certainly No Place for Bigotry in Reviews

Sometimes, a review may appear to include totally unacceptable bigotry. A bit of proofreading before submitting a review wouldn't be a bad idea:

"Our meal was spoiled due to the restaurant being full of midgets. We changed tables but the midgets kept following us. Finally we had to leave but we woke up the next morning covered in bites."

What's in a Name?

The name of a hotel or restaurant should give you some idea about what to expect, although it's understandable that some of these places may not always live up to the expectations their name creates.

Decent Hotel
OK, this hotel is not promising too much but at least it should provide acceptable accommodation:

"From outside it looks decent and well maintained but in reality it's a devil's den."

A bit harsh... How about another opinion?

"The moment you step in you feel dizzy vibes. Rooms were closed and I felt like a prisoner."

OK, maybe we'll skip the Decent Hotel and look for something more upmarket. How about the "Star Hotel"? Sounds very nice.

"This place is a very very basic one where customers are not bothered about amenities due to low price or who want to do some nasty stuff and leave."

Maybe this isn't for me, either.

Often, a hotel's name evokes a wonderful image that the hotel may not be able to live up to.

<u>Hotel Sunny Paradise</u>
This sounds lovely — I'm sure they wouldn't lie.

"very difficult to sleep - too much Miskito's at night".

Another reviewer said they stayed here because their car broke down nearby. *"A good place to stay in an emergency"*. I'll keep that in mind the next time my car breaks down in Mumbai.

There's actually a hotel on a Pacific island called "A Place to Remember". That's certainly asking for trouble with disgruntled reviewers. Review titles include:

"A Place to Avoid"
"A Place to Forget" — a particularly popular title
"A place to remember for all the wrong reasons" — also very popular

Sometimes, the name of an establishment doesn't try to fool you into thinking you're going to have a luxury experience. It may be surprising, but many people seem to legitimately enjoy their stay at the "Jail Hostel". This really is a 150-year-old prison that has been converted into a place to stay — even for those who have not (yet) committed any serious crimes.

The concept initially seems very cool and perhaps it's understandable that people think this could be a fun experience. In actual fact, the appeal of staying in a real prison can quickly wear off!

"The old jail has a bad atmosphere, because it is a place where people have suffered, even died, for ages. At the top floor is the death row and the gallows with the hanging rope."

"I booked one double room with window, bath, kitchenette and ended up in a real jail no window, no bath, nothing."

"Honestly it is not worth even staying the night for the experience because its not really an experience anyway. You can have the same experience sleeping in your closet at home and save the money, or for a real experience sleep in your bathroom with your dirty laundry beside you for the smell."

"The smell. I think there's something dead on level 4 and they didn't find it yet. The smell is really terrible. It's like old stinky cheesy feet, all over the place."

"Seems like a great idea and thought it would be cool and interesting. literally could not believe my eyes when I got to where I was meant to be spending the night. May seem like stating the obvious but it really is literally a CELL!"

Then there are some hotel names that simply leave you scratching your head:

- Jyoti Lunch Home
- Tulip Living Solution
- Corporate Shelters
- Apocalypse 22
- Hotel Planet Hollybum
- Let-You-Inn
- Dingdong Nuns
- Two Stupid Dogs
- Poo
- Red Boobies
- Badhotel
- Resist Bacteria Hotel

And you may want to think twice before visiting any of these (very real) restaurants:

- Khmer Fungus Noodle
- The Alleged Café
- Oh My Gosh!
- Soon Fatt
- McWanks
- Dancing Crap
- KKK
- Cabbages and Condoms
- Sprinkling chisa nyama and car-wash
- Mr. Piss
- My Dung
- Chocopocalypse
- The Cannibal Liquor House (may not be suitable for teetotal vegans)

Lost in Translation

As a native English speaker, it is certainly tempting to only read reviews written in English. The downside of this is you run the risk of missing out on unique perspectives and insights from people all around the world. Of course, if you don't speak any foreign languages you will need to rely on the dubious capabilities of an automatic translation function.

"In short very top, we took our legs to our neck after a salty note." — what?

"Noodles is food made by angels near the serving there. It is without doubt the worst food I've ever ingested in life. And it's not cheap, or will die anyway."

"Without infamy and without praise, it surprises you with the pizza dough which strangely is not a boat but it is indeed very light and lusteth lot!"

"The homemade tiramisu ... can give you a deep depression ..."

"Finally I want to say that all kinds of meatball think cheese cake is delicious in the end ye what's going on! Sour taste in the end to do very hard! Very recommended!"

Of course, translation challenges can also be the cause of many problems people encounter while on foreign travels:

"We went into Benidorm for day. On return asked for a kettle and cups that should have been provided. 30 minutes later we were presented with a mop and bucket?????????
It really wasn't funny at the time."

Paris

Paris is another of the world's great tourist destinations, and there are certainly many excellent restaurants in this fascinating city. But with more than 15,000 restaurants listed in online reviews, it is inevitable that there will be at least a few you should avoid. And more so when you consider the wonderful reputation that Parisian waiters have for their warmth and friendliness toward tourists and other non-French speakers (sarcasm?).

However, if you read reviews written in French, it becomes apparent that Parisian waiters don't reserve their rudeness for foreigners alone. And strangely enough, it seems the French often have a close association between rude waiters and comedy shows.

"bad food, not clean, no toilets. The worst of the worst, it's here. Special mention to the waitress so rude that one would think it was a comedy sketch."

"The waitress was so rude we were convinced there must be a hidden camera for a comedy show."

"Deplorable service and welcome. The manager is just odious and distills a tension that makes you feel uncomfortable. Flee this establishment that will not make you have a good time."

Review Titles Can Tell You All You Need to Know

Regardless of the language used, I have to admit that the vast majority of critical reviews are not particularly interesting or amusing to read. They tend to go on and on about the usual array of problems, including torn and stained sheets, dirty carpets, malfunctioning toilets and showers, bed bugs and cockroaches, grumpy waiters, overpriced drinks, and rancid food that plays havoc with your digestive system.

But very often, just reading the review titles can give you all the information you need about a particularly nasty establishment.

The following titles all come from reviews for the same hotel:

"This place is scary!"
"An Alfred Hitchcock movie set"
"Hell Hole"
"Don't come here, please!"
"Holocaust Camp"
"Barely made it out alive"
"Make sure you have said last words to your loved ones"
"This place gave my wife a horrible flashback 6 months after our very brief visit"

Try to See the Positive Side

After having waded through thousands of dreary, complaining reviews, I have to say I do love it when reviewers try to see the positive side of what they could have simply portrayed as a horrible experience.

"Oh, the 5 inch rat climbing up and down behind the bar (which shares a wall with the restaurant) was a nice touch."

"The journey through the alleyway to get to the hotel was an experience -- an open men's urinal complete with men urinating added a certain 'ambience' to the surroundings!"

"a good long wait to get a fisherman's pie that my eyes, my mouth and my bowels still remember"

"I have stayed at hostels outside of the country and used holes in the ground as toilets in 3rd world countries but these accommodations were much scarier. The room was smaller than 10x10 with cinder block cement walls. It was like a prison cell or asylum ward.... on the positive side, the diner turned out to have the best pancakes in town."

"The doors have been kicked in. There is blood on the door. The shower has large holes in the walls. The rooms are crawling with flies & roaches. Weirdly, the sheets are pristine & white."

From a review simply titled *"Stay Away!"*:

"DO NOT TURN OFF THE LIGHT! The moment you do, the walls will literally crawl with nasty little roaches. It's a horrid place to stay, but the Pizza Place next door is nice!"

And lastly, this review from somewhere in Central Africa:

"The lack of a toilet seat was immediately forgotten once I turned on the shower and watched sludge drip from the pipe / shower head on the ceiling. Then I was struck by movement on the tiles. On closer inspection I noted an entire biological experiment playing itself out on each tile - an ecosystem all of its own.

Giving up on the shower, I went to bed and it was then I noticed that the majority of window panes were missing. Just as well, as the air-con wasn't working. Nevertheless fatigue overcame me and I went to sleep.

What followed next can only be described as surreal. My entire bedroom exploded into a disco beat. My bed levitated from the floor as my room turned into a boom-box. I was located immediately above the hotel nightclub. It was at some time in the early morning that the music ended. This continued for the next few nights.

It was truly an unforgettable experience. Highly recommended to music aficionados and urban biologists."

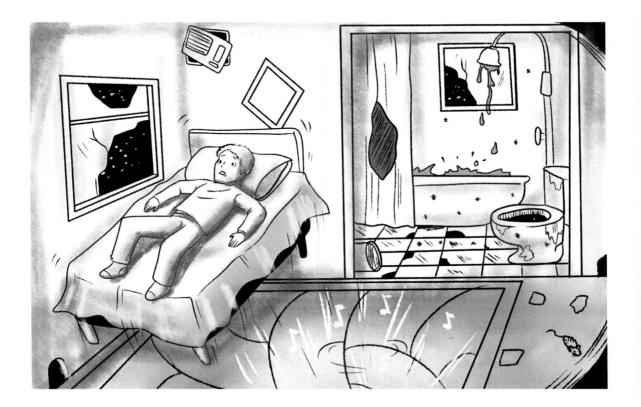

Final Thoughts

Through the process of researching for this book, I feel that I have travelled the world: everywhere from New York, Paris, and Tokyo to such exotic destinations as Pyongyang, Albania, and the remotest parts of Central Africa.

Unfortunately, with my focus on grim and disappointing travel experiences, I've become familiar with many of the worst places in the world. I've also visited many of the finest hotels and restaurants, but unfortunately accompanied by some of the most miserable people in the world.

Ultimately, I believe I can confidently say that it is possible to have a fantastic time travelling the world for fun and adventure. By all means, take full advantage of the wisdom and advice offered through the vast array of invaluable online travel reviews. But most importantly: be careful out there!